Silly Sketcher

I0867695

Draw Funny 3-D Pictures!

written by Luke Colins

illustrated by Catherine Cates

BLACK RABBIT BOOKS

Hi Jinx is published by Black Rabbit Books
P.O. Box 227, Mankato, Minnesota, 56002.
www.blackrabbitbooks.com

Jennifer Besel, editor; Catherine Cates, interior designer; Michael Sellner, cover designer; Omay Ayres, photo researcher

Library of Congress Cataloging-in-Publication Data
Names: Colins, Luke, author.
Title: Draw funny 3-D pictures! / by Luke Colins.
Description: Mankato, Minnesota : Black Rabbit Books, [2020] | Series: Hi jinx. Silly sketcher | Audience: Ages: 8-12. | Audience: Grades: 4 to 6. | Includes bibliographical references and index.
Identifiers: LCCN 2018037476 (print) | LCCN 2019000264 (ebook) | ISBN 9781680729535 (ebook) | ISBN 9781680729474 (library binding) | ISBN 9781644660720 (pbk.)
Subjects: LCSH: Perspective—Juvenile literature. | Drawing—Technique—Juvenile literature.
Classification: LCC NC750 (ebook) | LCC NC750 .C67 2020 (print) | DDC 741.2—dc23
LC record available at https://lccn.loc.gov/2018037476

Image Credits

Alamy: Matthew Cole, 5; iStock: carbouval, 5; Shutterstock: anfisa focusova, 19; designer_an, 12; Giuseppe_R, 5; Glinskaja Olga, 20; Mario Pantelic, Cover, Back Cover, 3, 5, 24, 25; Memo Angeles, Cover, 4, 5, 6, 11, 12, 13, 14, 17, 19, 20, 23; Olga Sabo, 2-3, 5; opicobello, 3, 13, 15, 19; owatta, 5; Pasko Maksim, Back Cover, 16; Pitju, 3, 7; Ron Dale, 3, 4, 5, 6, 8, 13, 15, 16, 19, 20; Tueris, 11
Every effort has been made to contact copyright holders for material reproduced in this book. Any omissions will be rectified in subsequent printings if notice is given to the publisher.

Contents

Chapter 1

Be a Silly Sketcher!

Drawing is fun. But it's even better when you can make people laugh with your drawings! Pictures that seem to pop off a page are the best. And they're not all that hard to do.

To get started, gather some supplies. Grab the basics, like paper and pencils. Don't forget your funny bone. Then just follow the steps. You'll have hilarious art in no time.

What You Need

Chapter 2

Put Your Pencil to the Paper

Let's start by getting used to drawing a 3-D shape. A simple cube is fun and great practice.

Step 1

Draw a square.

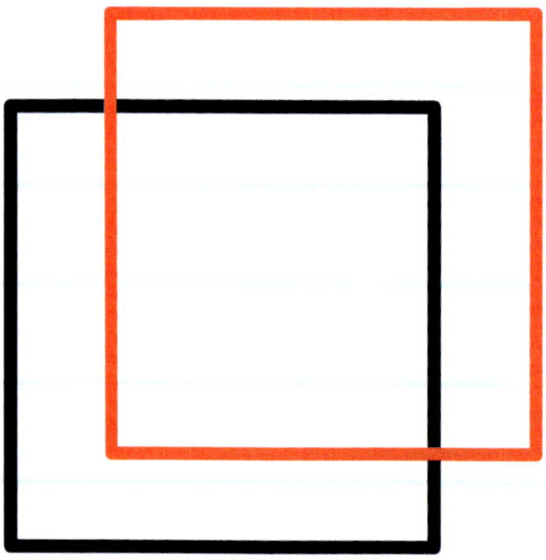

Step 2

Draw a second square **overlapping** the first one.

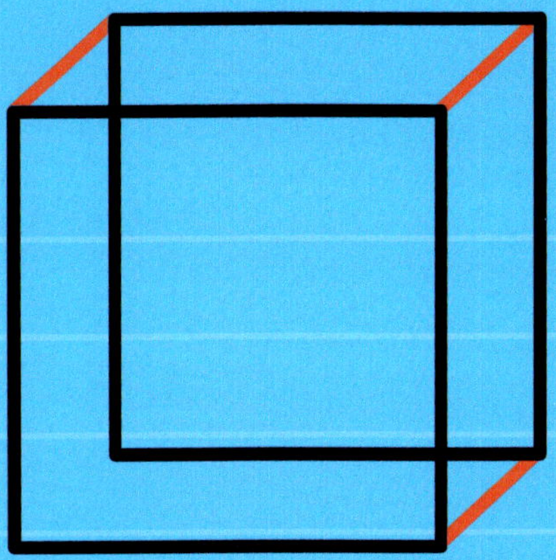

Step 3

Use straight lines to connect the corners of the squares.

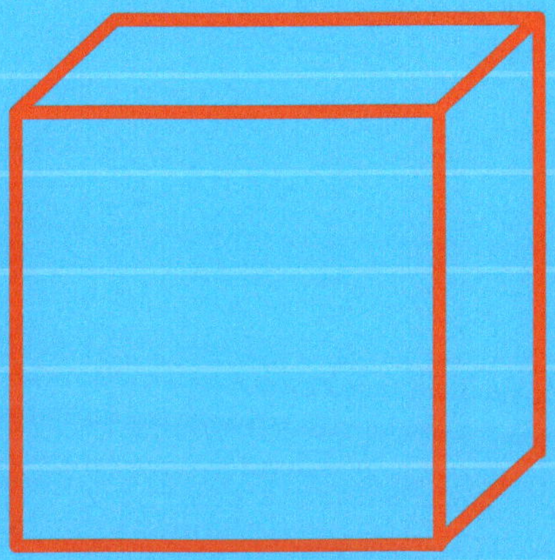

Step 4

Erase the lines inside the overlapping shapes.

Step 5

Color the cube however you'd like.

A Funny Fall

Falling down the stairs in real life isn't funny. But drawing it sure is!

Step 1

Start the stairs with straight and jagged lines. If you have trouble making the shapes, try **tracing** them first.

Step 2

Use a ruler to add straight lines. You'll already see the stairs taking shape.

Step 3

Draw more straight lines between the ones you just drew.

Finish It Up!

Use markers to **outline** your drawing. Then try colored pencils for **shading** it in.

Step 4

Use a jagged line to connect the stairs on the right side.

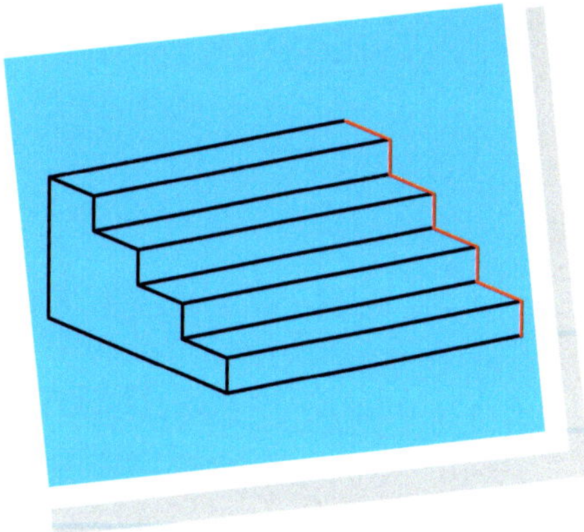

Step 5

Sketch in a falling stick figure.

Step 6

Erase the lines inside the overlapping shapes. And a dotted line to show movement.

Give Me a Hand

Trap your hand on paper.
Then watch the giggles get going.

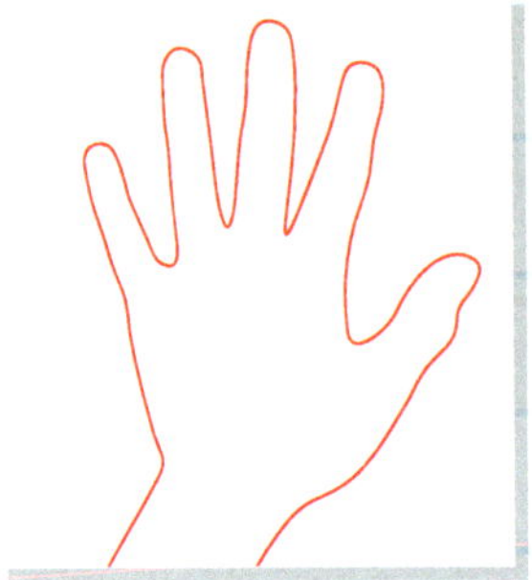

Step 1

Outline your hand on the paper. Draw lightly here. You'll erase these lines later.

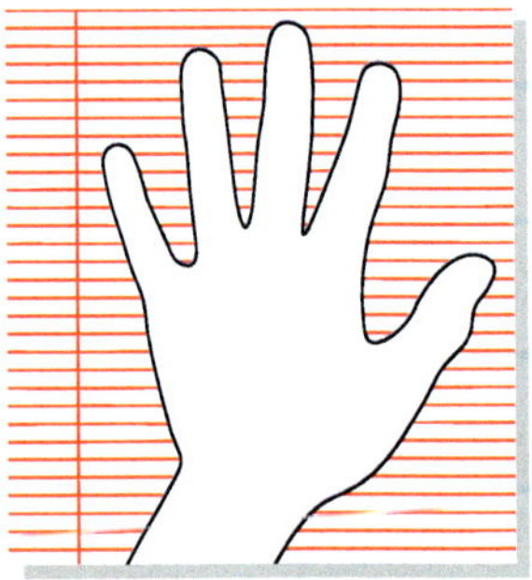

Step 2

Use a ruler to draw straight, even lines across the page. Don't draw lines inside the hand.

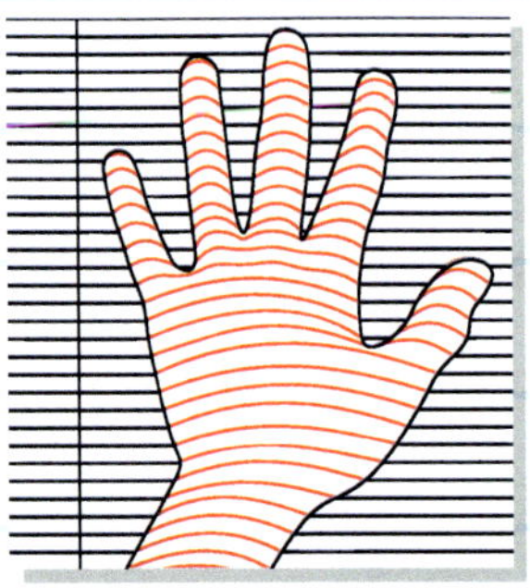

Step 3

Draw curved lines inside the hand. The beginning and end of each line should match up with the straight lines.

Step 4

Carefully erase the outline of the hand. Redraw any parts of the straight lines that might have been erased.

Step 5

Shade in shadows around the hand.

Shark Pond

What if you found sharks swimming in your park's pond? This drawing could be the start of a great story!

Step 1

Draw the curved outline of a pond.

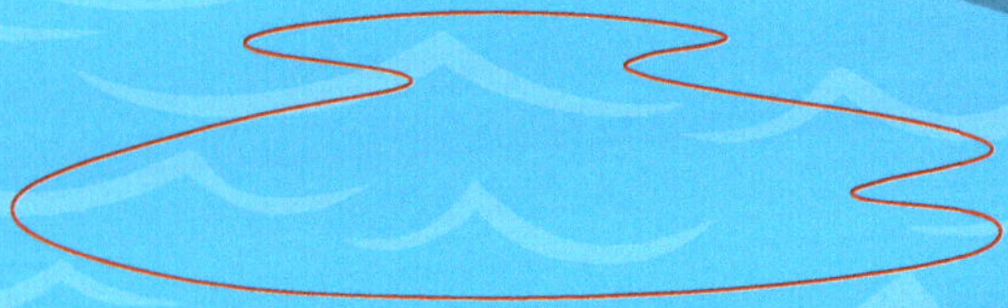

Step 2

Add detail lines inside the pond to give it a 3-D effect.

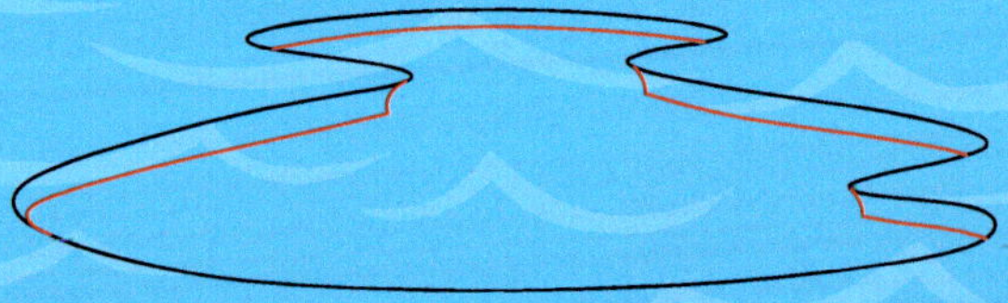

Step 3

Use curved lines to make the **illusion** of water.

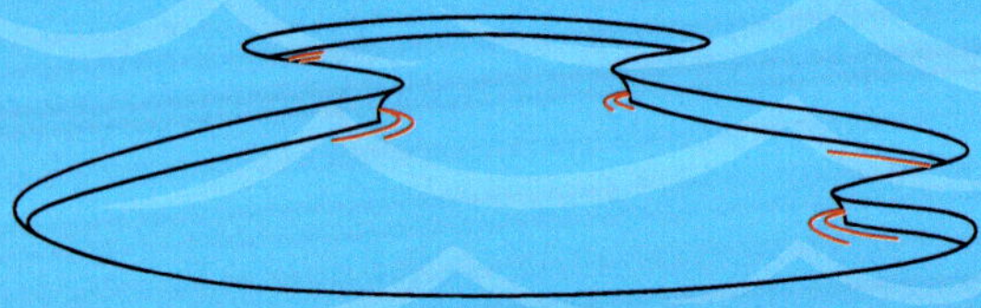

Finish It Up!

Put your drawing in a scene. Maybe add a playground and screaming kids.

Step 4

Draw in curved triangle shark fins.

Step 5

Erase the lines inside the overlapping shapes.

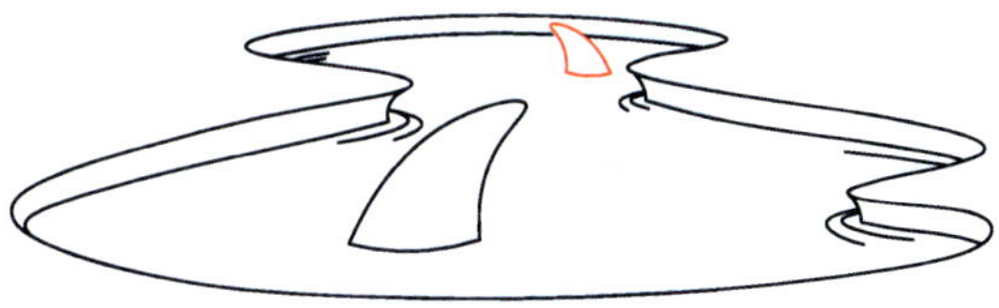

Step 6

Add more water lines around the fins.

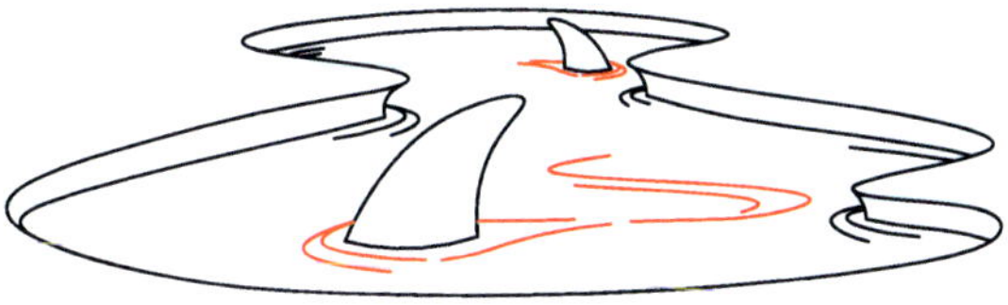

Climbing Cat

This cat looks like it's just hanging around your page.

Step 1

Use a ruler to draw evenly spaced lines across your page.

Step 2

Start the cat's head. Draw in front paws and the start of a body too.

Step 3

Add the lower part of the body and back paws.

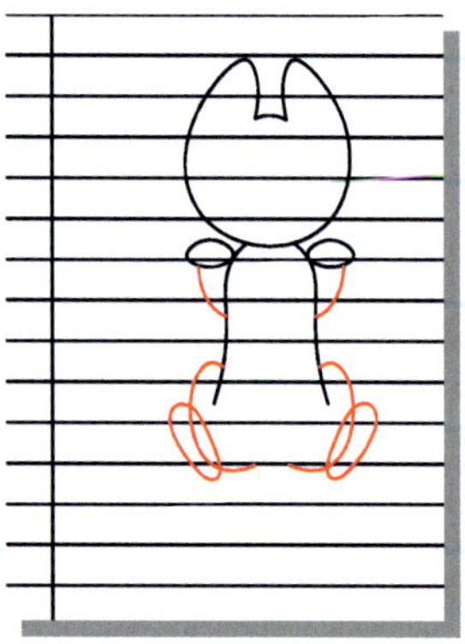

Step 4

Give the cat a tail and big eyes. Don't forget the extra comma shape for the tip of the tail.

Step 5

Erase the lines inside the overlapping shapes.

Step 6

Finish the cat's eyes. Give it a mouth and whiskers too.

Tip

Make sure to start the shapes so the paws and tail overlap the straight lines. That's the key to making it look like the cat is behind them.

Down the Rabbit Hole

Drawing this 3-D hole is simple and fun. Hop to it!

Step 1

Start by drawing a big oval.

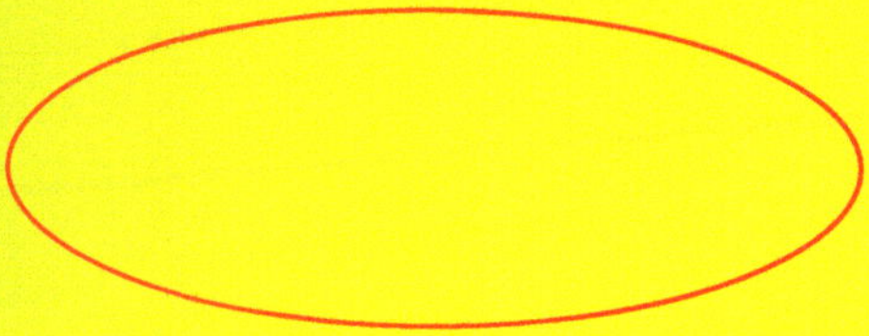

Step 2

Add several more ovals overlapping the first. The ovals should get **progressively** smaller. Make sure they all **align** on the bottom.

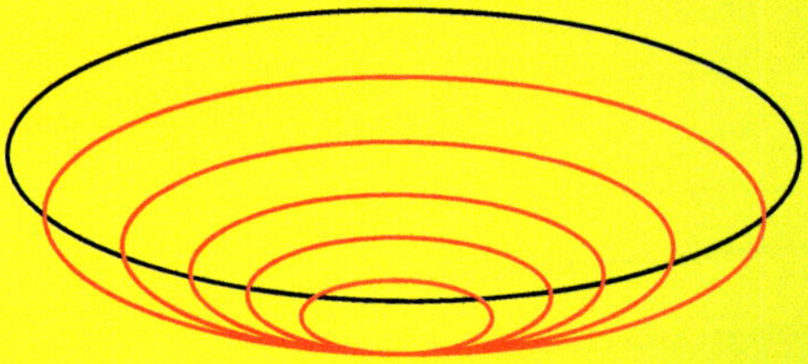

Step 3

Erase all the lines that go outside the original oval.

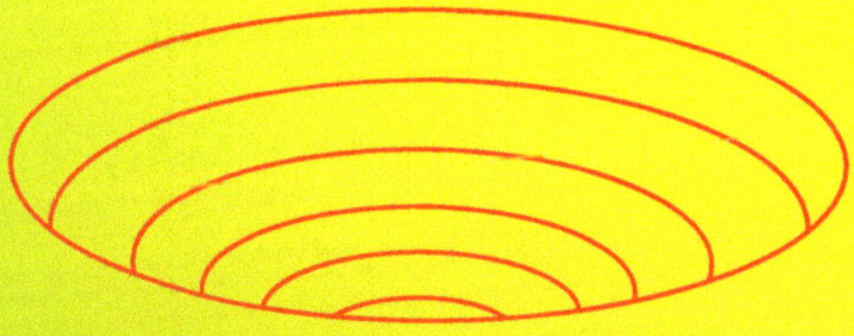

Finish It Up!

Shading adds a lot to a picture. Try adding some darker color to the edges of the hole. It will make it seem like the light disappears down the hole.

Step 4

Use two lopsided circles to start the rabbit.

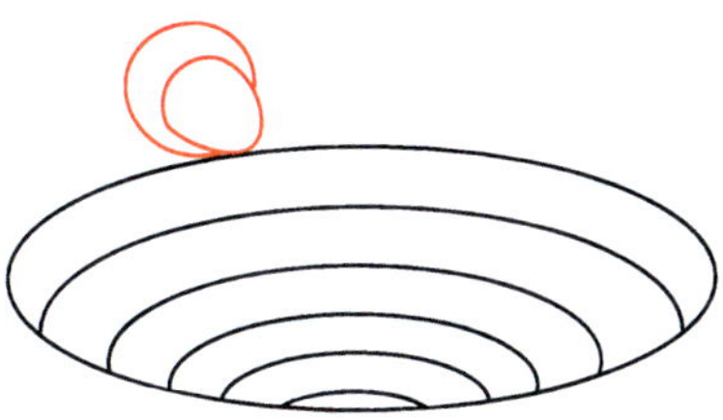

Step 5

Give the rabbit ears, paws, and a tail.

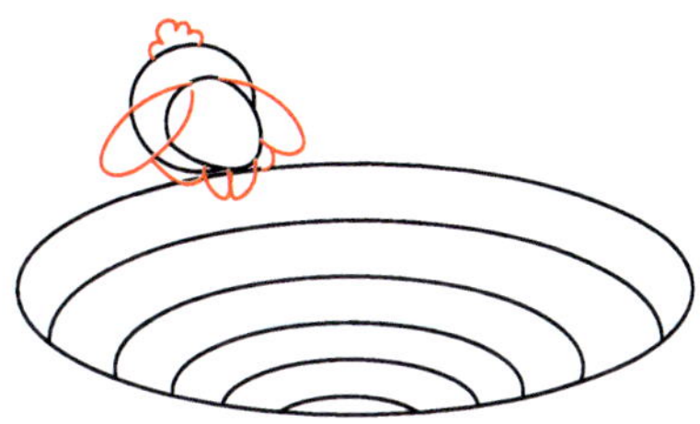

Step 6

Add big eyes and a nose. Put in **motion** lines too.

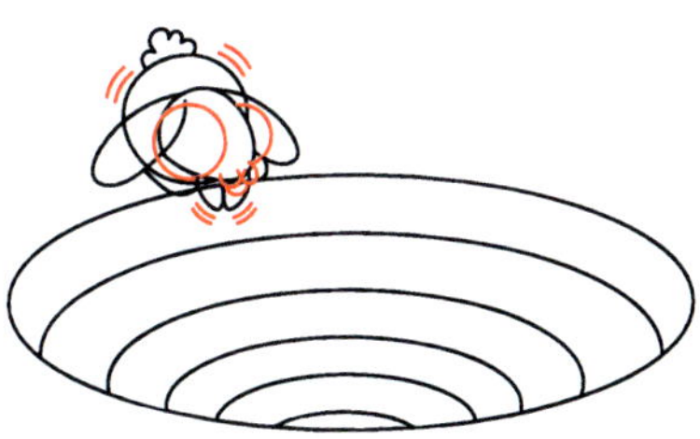

Step 7

Erase the lines inside the overlapping shapes. Then add **pupils**.

Just Hang On!

Bring characters on your page to life. You can have them falling off the page!

Step 1

Use a ruler to draw straight, even lines on your paper.

Step 2

Add curved lines in the middle of the page. Make sure the curved lines start and end on the straight lines.

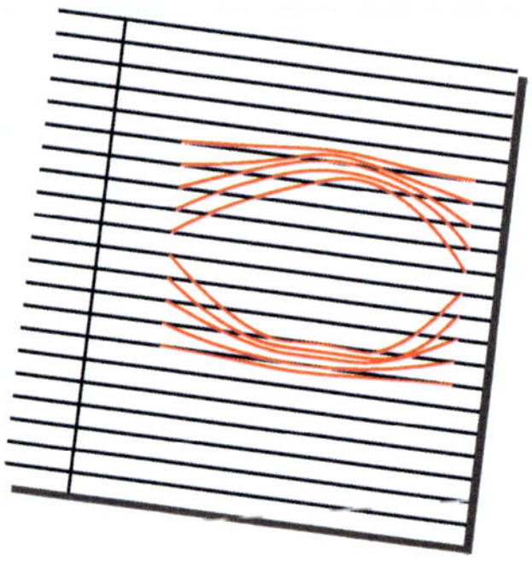

Step 3

Erase the straight lines underneath the curved ones. This will create the illusion of a hole. Redraw any parts of the straight lines that might have been erased.

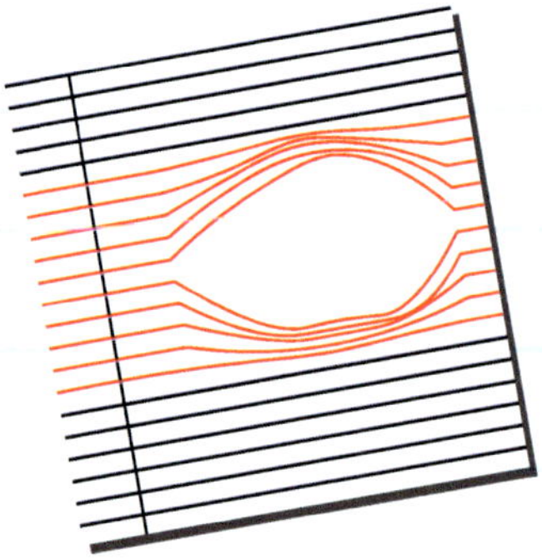

Step 4

Draw one stick figure in the hole. Make it look like it's holding the hole open. Add another stick figure dangling from the hole.

Step 5

Erase the lines inside the overlapping shapes. Then add motion lines.

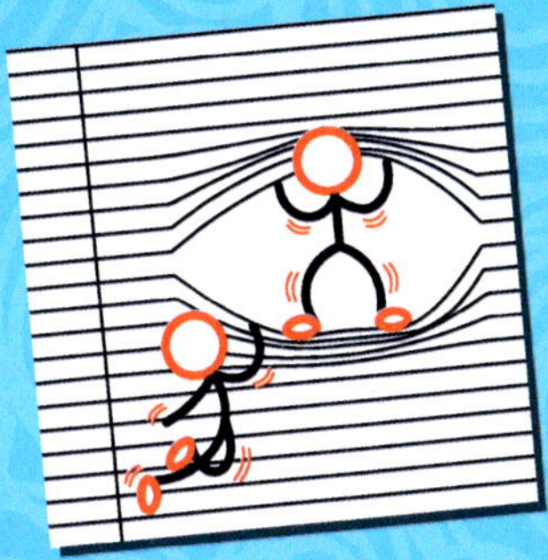

Tip

Add silly faces to the figures for even more laughs.

Chapter 3

Get in on the Hi Jinx

Book illustrators use the same steps you just did! They use simple shapes to build the frames of their drawings. Then they add details to make the drawings pop off the page. Maybe one day you'll illustrate a book!

Take It One Step More

1. Most of the drawings tell you to erase the lines inside overlapping shapes. What happens if you skip that step?

2. Are your sketches more or less funny with color? Why?

3. What features make these drawings funny?

GLOSSARY

align (uh-LYN)—to arrange things so they form a line or are in proper position

illusion (il-LOO-zhun)—something that looks or seems different from what it is

motion (MO-shun)—an act or process of moving

outline (AHWT-lyn)—to draw a line around the edges of something

overlap (oh-vur-LAP)—to extend over or past

progressively (pro-GREH-siv-lee)—increasing in extent or degree

pupil (PYU-pul)—the part of the eye that lets light in; in people, it's the round, black part of the eye.

shading (SHAY-ding)—the use of marking made within outlines to give a 3-D look, shadow, or degrees of light and dark in a drawing

trace (TRAYS)—to copy something by following the lines or letters as seen through a transparent sheet on top

LEARN MORE

BOOKS

Bergin, Mark. *Draw 3-D.* Step-by-Step. Brighton, England: Book House, 2018.

Kennedy, Nia. *Drawing a Horse with Rectangles.* Drawing with Shapes Is Fun! New York: PowerKids Press, 2019.

Let's Draw Aliens and Spaceships with Crayola! Let's Draw with Crayola! Minneapolis: Lerner Publications, 2019.

WEBSITES

Drawing for Kids
mocomi.com/fun/arts-crafts/drawing-for-kids/

How to Draw
www.hellokids.com/r_12/drawing-for-kids/

How to Draw Archives
www.artforkidshub.com/how-to-draw/

TIPS AND TRICKS

Make sure to let the marker outlines dry before coloring in your drawings.

Colored pencils are a great tool for coloring in your drawings. Layer a color over another for a cool blended effect.

Don't have a ruler handy? That's OK. Use any straight edge you can find. A piece of paper works pretty well.

Don't worry if your drawings don't look exactly like the ones in this book! Art is all about creating your own thing. Just have fun!